WM. H. Fleming
Augusta, Ga.

SLAVERY AND THE RACE PROBLEM IN THE SOUTH.

WITH SPECIAL REFERENCE TO THE STATE OF GEORGIA.

Address of William H. Fleming, Before the Alumni Society of the State University, Athens, June 19, 1906.

INTRODUCTION.

A concise statement of the reasons which led to this publication in a permanent form may appropriately be in the nature of a Publisher's Announcement, and excerpts from correspondence relating to it will probably give the best idea of these reasons.

The correspondence regarding this speech began by a letter from the writer, of which the following is a copy:

"July 5th 1906.

" Honorable William H. Fleming,
My Dear Mr. Fleming :—
I think that you and the whole country are to be congratulated upon your grand exposition of the principles which should guide the South, and indeed the whole country, in dealing with the problem of the negro race.

I have for several years spent my winters in Africa, and have studied the conditions of the African upon his own ground, having penetrated to the equatorial countries of the Uganda and the Congo State, in addition to traveling the whole extent of the Soudan, and while I agree with you in your statement that " God knows the South wants no more of that curse," of slavery, and while I agree with the general statement that " slavery is the sum of all evils," I have come to the conclusion that the greatest wrong which slavery inflicts upon a people is not upon the slave, but upon the *slaveholder*. No matter how greatly the slave is degraded, the evil effects to the superior race that holds the slave is in my opinion the greater wrong of the two to the general civilization of the world.

To be, as you are, a leader in this movement, is in my opinion one of the highest honors to which any American can aspire. I deem your speech a real milestone in the path of progress, and with your consent, I should be glad to reprint it in an attractive form to extend its circulation as far as I can.

Yours sincerely,
DANA ESTES."

A prompt reply contained the consent to the publication, and in offering it to the public, the editor felt that the endorsement of the leaders of political and moral movements throughout the country would be of service in extending its influence. He, therefore, addressed President Roosevelt for this purpose, and the following are excerpts from the correspondence regarding this subject:

"July 23rd, 1906.

" TO THE PRESIDENT,
My Dear Sir :—
I think it beyond doubt that your attention has been attracted to the patriotic and important speech of the Honorable William H. Fleming of Georgia.

I have asked of him, as per enclosed copy of my letter to him of July 5th, the privilege of reprinting this in an attractive form to extend its benefits as widely as possible. It seems to me to mark an epoch in this agitation, and I am informed that since the delivery of this speech the Committee of the Georgia legislature has reported against the passage of the disfranchisement bill without a dissenting vote. I believe this to be largely the result of Mr. Fleming's great speech.

If it would be entirely proper for you, in view of your exalted official position, to commend the sentiments of this speech, and permit such commendation to be used in an introduction to the speech, I should be pleased to receive the same from you.

The publication of the speech is not intended as a commercial transaction. * * * * *

Yours respectfully,
DANA ESTES."

(Hon. HARRY HAMMOND, Beach Island, S. C., letter June 27th.)

"Van Holst, a northern sympathizer, said a century and a half must elapse before a verdict could be reached as to the wisdom of emancipation. The solution of the race problem advocated by you — Justice to the Negro — needs no time for its confirmation. It is registered among the indisputable truths of eternity itself."

(Former Congressman WM. H. FELTON, Cartersville, Ga.)

"I thank you with all my heart for the address made at the Athens Commencement. Yours were words of sober caution and profound prudential wisdom."

(EMORY SPEER, U. S. District Judge, letter June 27th.)

"I have received the pamphlet print of your great speech on Slavery and the Race Problem in the South. I had the happiness of hearing this appeal to the intelligence and sense of justice of our people, and I cannot well overstate the pleasure it gave me to see with what enthusiasm the Alumni body of our Alma Mater present received such a fearless and truthful exposition of great and salutary truths."

(JAMES R. RANDAL, New Orleans, Author of "Maryland, My Maryland," letter June 27th.)

"The speech was a masterpiece. No one else could have done it."

(Judge W. H. HULSEY, Atlanta, Ga., letter June 29th.)

"Reading your address from start to finish, it pleases me to say that every patriotic Georgian ought to feel grateful to you for giving to your state a clear, forceful and masterly presentation in your Athens address of what may be termed the Negro Problem."

(Hon. MOORFIELD STOREY, Boston, Mass., letter June 29th.)

"It is a courageous thing to stand up in one's country and speak as you have done, and such courage is very much needed today. You have never lacked that quality, and I hope your example will be an inspiration to others."

"Oyster Bay, N. Y., July 25, 1906.

"My Dear Mr. Estes:

I am glad that you are to publish ex-Congress-man Fleming's noteworthy speech in more permanent form than it is possible ordinarily to publish such speeches. * * * * *

Mr. Fleming's speech is admirable, alike for its fearlessness, its sanity, and the high purpose which it shows. The problems of any one part of our great common country should be held to be the problems of all our country — at least to the extent that all our people should give their hearty and respectful sympathy to those who in their own neighborhood, are trying to solve their particular problems aright. In each locality we have our own special and peculiar difficulties; and when a brave and honest man does good work in meeting the peculiar difficulties of his own region, he not only does good therein, but by example and influence he helps Americans in other parts of our great common-wealth manfully to grapple with the various evils which they in their turn, have to strive against.

Sincerely yours,

THEODORE ROOSEVELT."

At the writer's especial request, Mr. Fleming has fur-nished him with a few excerpts from the many letters of approval which he has received from all parts of the coun-try; and especially from leaders of opinion in the South. In his reply he says: "Many of the strongest commenda-tions which my speech have received have been given to me in person by word of mouth, and, consequently, do not appear in written form that could be used." Among the many received by letters may be quoted the following from Judge John L. Hopkins of Atlanta:

"I have read your speech more than once. It is satisfying. In some of its parts it has been comforting to me — in all, inter-esting. The preparation of such a paper is a valuable service to the state. It was needed — it was just the right thing."

(Judge JOEL BRANHAN of Rome, Ga., letter June 23rd.)

"I want to thank you for your grand speech on the disfranchisement of the negro before the Alumni of the University of Georgia on the 19th inst., which I have just had the pleasure of reading. It is truthful, honest and unanswerable."

(R. F. CAMPBELL, Ashville, N. C., letter June 25th.)

"In intellectual strength and moral soundness, it takes the place easily among the very best things ever written or spoken on this subject."

(Congressman W. M. HOWARD, Atlanta, Ga., letter June 25th.)

"I am very glad to get the speech, not because it is a revelation to me of your views on this question, but especially to know precisely what you said in view of the criticism I have seen in the papers about it. The speech is up to the very best of your ability, and I am proud of you as a friend and a citizen of Georgia because of the pertinence and power of the speech. I am glad that you made it when and where you did. It is the strongest and clearest voice that has been heard since this issue became state wide."

(Prof. W. S. BEAN, Clinton, S. C., letter June 25th.)

"I am delighted with the address, its calmness and fairness of statement, its ample basis of fact, its appeal to a sense of justice and fairness and its belief in the principle that no wrong can be inflicted for political purposes which will not certainly react upon the agent at sometime. * * * * * I am glad you had such a splendid opportunity, such a fine, intelligent audience, and that you rose to the occasion in a speech that is masterly, statesmanlike and Christian. May you live long to keep up such a good work and find staunch friends to stand by you and your principles."

(C. P. GOODYEAR, Brunswick, Ga., letter June 27th.)

"That was a great and statesmanlike and patriotic speech of yours at the University. The day will come when wise men in Georgia, — good men everywhere, — will appreciate the calm temper and patriotic thought which dictated it."

9

(GEORGE FOSTER PEABODY, New York City, letter June 28th.)

"The more I think of the matter, the more do I believe that you have done a far-reaching service and that it may well prove to be the case that no address during the last twenty years has been more important."

(Ex-Gov. ALLEN D. CANDLER, Atlanta, Ga., letter July 4th.)

"I have read it with a great deal of interest, and it is without exaggeration a gem, and every loyal Georgian who knows Georgia and her career in the past and the apparent insuperable obstacles her people have had to surmount will thank you for it. * * * I think no fitter occasion could have been found for the utterance of the lofty sentiments contained in it than the Commencement of the State University before the Alumni Association of the oldest state college in America."

(T. C. BETTERTON, Dalton, Ga., letter July 8th.)

"Please allow me to say that you have in this address performed the highest possible service to your state and to the South. I would that every citizen in our state could read it thoroughly."

(Rev. WALKER LEWIS, Augusta, Ga., letter July 15th.)

"I have just finished the best Sunday reading I have seen in many years. It is your great article on the Race Question. It is masterful, it is unanswerable, it is worthy of a great statesman; it is Christian philosophy and righteousness."

(FRANCIS LYNDE STETSON, Sterlington, Rockland Co., N. Y., letter July 8th.)

"I consider it the best presentation of the various phases of this difficult question that I have ever seen, and his proposed solution through the ordinary observation of the universal mandate of the moral law attests his sanity."

"Lake George, N. Y., 3rd July, 1906.
"THE HONORABLE WILLIAM H. FLEMING, Augusta, Ga.
My Dear Sir : —
I cannot forbear writing to you of my delight at your great speech, delivered before the Alumni Society

at the University of Georgia. In its insight, its iron logic, its political perspective, and its high morality, it is, I think, one of the greatest constructive addresses of the time ; and these qualities mark it as belonging to that class of political literature to which the speeches of Webster, Hayne and Lincoln belong. I would not be guilty of flattery, but such an address at such a time and place is an event which gives one a legitimate pride in human kind, and a joy in the mere fact of living. I have long felt that this time with its problems, on the principle that great occasions make great men, is one which must call into being and action men of the first order, men who are capable of seeing the significance of the time and of meeting its great demands. I think the men are coming, and I hail your speech as a sign that they are coming.   Faithfully yours,

SAMUEL H. BISHOP."

(Prof. CHAS. ELIOT NORTON, Cambridge, Mass., letter Aug. 11th.)

"Nothing could be better than its spirit. It would be a most encouraging sign in these confused days should your appeal to the intelligent and moral sympathy of the community be heeded and responded to."

(RICHARD C. OGDEN, Madison Ave., New York, letter Aug. 12th.)

"I appreciate your great contribution to the solution of the one great question that retards the growth of American unity."

(H. B. BROWN, Ex-Justice Sup. Court, U. S., letter Aug. 5th.)

"I cannot refrain from expressing to you my appreciation of your masterly address of June 19th upon Slavery and the Race Problem. It is quite the most satisfactory of any I have seen upon that subject. I cannot doubt your views will ultimately prevail in the South, as they do already in the North. I have always believed the question of suffrage would finally be solved by the adoption of an educational or property qualification, which, if fairly administered, would answer the purpose. I do not think anyone should be disfranchised solely on account of color."

The writer has made no attempt to collect the opinions

of the Press, though he has seen many that were as emphatic in commendation as are the personal opinions herewith submitted. He can not, however, refrain from a brief excerpt from an editorial of the "Augusta (Ga.) Chronicle:"

"The speech was pronounced by all who heard it or read it to be the greatest ever delivered from the University platform."

It may not be inappropriately stated that commercial considerations have had no part in influencing the publication of this speech, that the profits arising from its publication will be devoted to educational work in the South, and that the editor, and not the author, is responsible for the insertion of the quotations on page facing the title page of the work, and the portrait of the author.

DANA ESTES.

SLAVERY AND THE RACE PROBLEM IN THE SOUTH.

Brothers of the Alumni Society, Ladies and Gentlemen:

It is my purpose to discuss slavery and the race problem in the South, with special reference to our own State of Georgia.

No public issue is more deserving of thoughtful consideration by our people, and no occasion could be more fit for its discussion. This audience is qualified in head and heart to appreciate at its true value every argument that may be advanced, and this platform at our chief seat of learning is so lifted up, that words spoken here may be heard in all parts of the State, echoing among the "Hills of Habersham" and over the "Sea Marshes of Glynn."

If there be any one present perturbed by a secret doubt as to the propriety of my bringing this subject and this occasion together in the midst of the pending political campaign in Georgia, let me hasten to allay his fears with the assurance that I shall carefully refrain from all offensive

9

personal allusions. Speaking to this very point some weeks before his fatal illness, Chancellor Hill cordially approved of my selection of the race problem for discussion at this time before the alumni of the university, and he added with characteristic broadmindedness: "I wish my platform at Athens to be a place for the freest expression of honest thought."

At the outset, we should realize that if we are to make any genuine progress toward a right solution of our problem, we must approach it in a spirit of the utmost candor, and with an eye single to the ascertainment of the truth. The pessimist "sailing the Vesuvian Bay" listens for the dreaded rumblings of the distant mountain—blind to the wondrous beauties of earth and sky about him. The optimist floating down the placid upper stream pictures to himself an endless panorama of peaceful landscapes—deaf to the thundering cataract of Niagara just below him. But better than pessimism and better than optimism is that philosophy which faces facts as they are, and courageously interprets their meaning.

Slavery and Christianity.

In the earlier civilizations slavery was the rule, not the exception. But with the advent of the Christ and His teachings, a silent, gentle, yet all-compelling force began its work on the universal heart of humanity. Christianity adjusted itself to existing governmental institutions, including slavery. But it inculcated such lofty doctrines of love and duty, and created such vivid conceptions of a personal God and Father of us all, that it was only a question of time when Christian peoples could not hold in slavery those of their own faith and blood.

In England in 1696 the doctrine had obtained wide acceptance that Christian baptism of itself worked a legal manumission of the slave. Argument to that effect was urged by able lawyers in the court of King's Bench in the suit of Chamberlain v. Herney, but the case went off on another ground, and that point was not decided. About the same time, however, the colonies of Maryland, Virginia and South Carolina passed laws that Christian baptism should not free the negro slave, "any opinion or matter to the contrary notwithstanding." Thus we see a recognition of the necessity at that period of our history of controlling by statutory enactments this expanding sentiment of Christian brotherhood among the masses of the people, so as to prevent it from embracing the alien negro race.

The march of Christian civilization had put an end to white slavery, but negro slavery still flourished, chiefly because the negro was of a different race-blood from his masters. Oneness in faith and blood had grown to mean freedom for the white man. But oneness in faith, without oneness in blood, still meant slavery for the negro.

Indeed, negro slavery as a historical institution in Western civilization occupies a unique position of its own. It began in the fifteenth century when white slavery had practically ceased. Most other slaveries were incidental results of wars. Negro slavery originated in commerce, in trade and barter, and so continued until it was suppressed.

Justification of Negro Slavery Based on Race-Inferiority.

When in later years the institution was summoned before the bar of the world's public opinion, its most logical and profound defenders admitted the wrongfulness of white slavery, but justified negro slavery on the plea of the natural inferiority of the negro race.

Alexander Stephens, then vice-president of the Southern Confederacy, in his famous Corner-Stone Speech at Savannah in March, 1861, said: "Many governments have been founded upon the principle of subordination and serfdom of certain classes of the same race. Such were, and are, in violation of the laws of nature. Our system contains no such violation of nature's laws. With us, all the white race, however high or low, rich or poor, are equal in the eye of the law. Not so with the negro; subordination is his place." * * * * Referring to the Confederacy, he declared: "Its foundations are laid, its corner stone rests, upon the great truth that the negro is not equal to the white man, that slavery — subordination to the superior race — is his natural and normal condition."

The fact of race inequality here stated cannot well be denied. But there is still a fatal flaw in the logic. That flaw lies in the assumption that a superior race has the right to hold an inferior race in slavery. A race can not be justly deprived of liberty merely because it is relatively inferior to another. If so, all other branches of the human family could justly be reduced to slavery by the highest, most masterful branch — and that mastery could only be determined by force of arms. The obligation of the superior to lead and direct does not carry with it the right to enslave.

Mr. Stephens further declared in his speech: "It is upon this, as I have stated, our social fabric is firmly planted, and I can not permit myself to doubt the ultimate

13

success of the full recognition of this principle throughout the civilized and enlightened world."

Here we have one of the ablest intellects of his day not only asserting that negro slavery was legally and morally right, but predicting that its recognition would become universal throughout the civilized world—a prediction made within five years of its abolition in the United States, and within twenty-seven years of its abolition in Brazil, which marked the final disappearance of human slavery as a legalized institution among civilized peoples.

Let me say in passing, that this Corner-Stone speech is not to be found in the authorized volume containing the biography and speeches of Mr. Stephens. One can scarcely suppress the question: Did the great commoner prefer for posterity to judge him by other speeches? Certain it is, that the views he expressed on negro slavery did not spring from hardness of heart, or want of sympathy with any suffering creature on earth. At his death, his negro body servant in tearful accents pronounced upon him this noble eulogy: "Mars Alec was kinder to dogs than most men is to folks."

But Mr. Stephens was defending the then existing institution of slavery handed down to his people by their

14

fathers, recognized by historical analogies from the Bible, and sanctioned by the Federal Constitution. His moral nature was uncompromising. There was no way to adjust that moral nature to existing conditions except by making the assumption, which he did make, of the right of a superior race to enslave an inferior race.

If race environment could so warp the judgment of a great intellect like that of Alexander Stephens, other men may well be cautious lest they miss the truth.

We need not stop to discuss whether the North or South was the more responsible for negro slavery in America. It takes two to make a bargain. Northern traders sold and Southern planters bought. If Charleston, South Carolina, was one of the chief ports of destination for slave trading vessels, Salem, Massachusetts, was one of the chief ports from whence those vessels sailed.

In the earlier days of the Southern colonies there were many strong protests against negro slavery. But once established it continued to grow and flourish until we reached those unhappy days foreshadowed by Mr. Madison, when he said in the constitutional convention of 1787 that the real antagonism would not arise between the large States on the one hand and the small States on the other, as many seemed to fear, but that "The institution of

15

slavery and its consequences formed the line of discrimination."

Slavery the Irritating Cause of the War.

No historian can ever truthfully assert that the men who bore the banner of the Confederacy in victory and in defeat with such matchless courage and heroic sacrifice were moved only by the selfish purpose of holding their black fellowmen in bondage. They were inspired by the noblest sentiments of patriotism. So far from being traitors to the Constitution of their fathers, which Mr. Gladstone declared was the "most wonderful work ever struck off at a given time by the brain and purpose of man," they reverenced that great instrument next to the Bible. So far from trampling it under foot, they held it up as their shield. They appealed to the North and West to recognize the binding obligation of that Constitution, as interpreted by the highest court, only to hear it denounced at last as "a covenant with death and an agreement with hell."

And yet, we must in candor admit that the truthful historian will write it down that slavery was the particular irritating cause that forced on the conflict of arms between the sections, though deeper causes lay at the foundation of our sectional differences on centralization and State rights.

When Robert Toombs made his memorable farewell speech in the United States Senate on January 7, 1861, he laid down five propositions, setting forth the contentions of the South, which, if granted, would have averted disunion. Every one of those five propositions was a clear cut, logical deduction from the original meaning and intent of the Constitution, and all five of them centred around the institution of slavery.

Again, when the conflict was over and the Constitution was amended at three separate times, two of these amendments, the thirteenth and fifteenth, referred exclusively to slavery, and the other, the fourteenth, referred chiefly to slavery. No other historical facts, though there are many, need to be cited to prove that slavery was the immediate precipitating cause of the Civil War.

The Thirteenth Amendment.

The thirteenth amendment, ratified in 1865, abolishing slavery, was a legitimate and necessary result of the arbitrament of the sword. Mr. Lincoln at first declared that the purpose of the war, on the part of the government, was to preserve the Union and not to free the slaves. But the progress of events had rendered him powerless to confine the struggling forces of social upheaval within that limitation—even if his personal views had undergone no change.

Great was the relief to many thoughtful minds in the South when this fruitful cause of sectional contention had been removed. In an address delivered from this platform in 1871, Benjamin H. Hill gave thanks in fervid metaphor that the "dusky Helen" had left the crumbling walls of Troy, and that Southern genius, once "bound like Prometheus" to the rock of slavery, had been loosed from its bonds.

The Fourteenth Amendment.

The fourteenth amendment, ratified in 1868, was a combination of judicial wisdom in the first section, of fruitless compromise in the second section, and of political proscription in the third section.

The first section of this amendment must now be regarded as one of the very best parts of the entire instrument. It gave for the first time an authorative definition of United States citizenship, and forbade any state to abridge the privileges of such citizens or to deprive any person of life, liberty or property without due process of law, or to deny to any person within its jurisdiction the equal protection of the laws. We had lived nearly three-quarters of a century under a government that had no constitutional or statutory definition of its own citizenship, and with no sufficient jurisdiction in its courts to give adequate protection to the equal rights now attaching to that citizenship.

What constituted one a citizen of the United States had long been a subject of discussion in the public journals, in the executive departments and in the courts. The Supreme Court, in the Dred Scott case in 1857, decided that a person of African descent, whether slave or free, was not, and could not be a citizen of a State or of the United States. That decision was, of course, superceded by the fourteenth amendment.

This first section was profound in its wisdom and far-reaching in its effect upon the rights of life, liberty and property, not only of blacks but of whites. That eminent Southern jurist, the Hon. Hannis Taylor, referring specially to this section, has well said: "From a purely scientific point of view the Constitution of the United States never reached its logical completion until after the adoption of the fourteenth amendment."

The omission from the original Constitution of a definition of United States citizenship and of a distinct provision against State encroachment on equal rights attaching thereto, carried with it a deep significance.

19

Few facts in our history point more unerringly to the conclusion that in the minds of the framers of that instrument, the paramount allegiance of the citizen was to his State, and not to the United States. It was this sense of duty which properly constrained Lee and other lovers of the Union to surrender their high commissions in the Federal army and cast their fortunes with their own seceding States. Happily, the future holds for us no possibility of the recurrence of that divided allegiance.

Historically, under the Constitution, the South was right, both as to slavery and secession, but the simple truth is that public opinion on those two subjects had outgrown the Constitution.

No man contributed more to the development of public opinion against disunion than did Mr. Webster. When he made his great speech in 1830 in reply to Mr. Hayne, closing with that matchless tribute to the Union flag: "The broad ensign of the Republic, now known and honored throughout the world, still full high advanced" — he created and vitalized and electrified Union sentiment throughout the length and breadth of the land. That speech, more than the word or deed of any other one man, prepared the way for the coming of Lincoln, and made possible the vast armies of Grant. After all, should not

Webster be given first place in the Hall of Fame dedicated to Saviors of the Union?

The Fifteenth Amendment.

The fifteenth amendment, ratified in 1872, prohibited the United States or any State, in prescribing suffrage qualifications, from discriminating against citizens of the United States on account of race, color or previous condition of servitude. It did not confer the ballot upon any one—it only prohibited discrimination on account of a specified difference. The right to vote is not a privilege or attribute of national citizenship under either the fourteenth or fifteenth amendment; but the right to be exempt from discrimination in voting on account of race is an attribute of national citizenship under the fifteenth amendment.

This amendment was at the time of its adoption a doubtful and dangerous experiment—but once made, it is beyond recall.

It embodied a distinct addition to the principle set out in the second section to the fourteenth amendment, which latter impliedly permitted a State to deny the ballot to the negro if it were willing to suffer the penalty of a proportionate reduction of representation in the lower house of Congress.

21

So far as the negro is concerned, the second section of the fourteenth amendment was a political compromise against him, while the fifteenth amendment was a complete declaration of his equal suffrage rights.

A resolution for a fourteenth amendment, in almost the identical words finally used in this second section in 1868, had been up for discussion in the Senate as early as 1866. Charles Sumner then denounced it as "a compromise of human rights, the most immoral, indecent and utterly shameful of any in our history."

Mr. Blaine, in his book, "Twenty Years in Congress," took the position that the enactment of the fifteenth amendment operated as a practical repeal of the second section of the fourteenth amendment. He says: "Before the adoption of the fifteenth amendment, if a State should exclude the negro from suffrage the next step would be for Congress to exclude the negro from the basis of apportionment. After the adoption of the fifteenth amendment, if a State should exclude the negro from suffrage, the next step would be for the Supreme Court to declare the act was unconstitutional and therefore null and void."

Some latter-day statesmen, who have introduced bills in Congress to reduce Southern representation, do not seem to agree with Mr. Blaine.

Verily, if the party of Sumner should ever abandon the vindication of the fifteenth amendment by substituting for it the compromise of the fourteenth amendment, the shade of that eminent statesman would surely be moved to indignation and contempt—if it still concerns itself with mundane political affairs. Such a substitute-compromise now could bring no good to either whites or blacks of the South. It would work evil and evil only.

Some Reasons for Adopting the Fifteenth Amendment.

The fifteenth amendment was naturally received with much bitterness by the white people of the South, because many of them interpreted it to mean that our political enemies of the North, who held control of the government, intended thereby to doom the South to perpetual negro domination.

No doubt many of such advocates were moved by prejudice and hate, but we of the South, in this day, must not blind ourselves to the fact that this amendment was advocated by some men then in public life who were not controlled by such base motives, but were patriotically striving to settle a great fundamental question of government on an enduring basis.

Let us not forget that when Congress passed the joint resolution submitting the fifteenth amendment to the States for adoption, the negroes had already been made citizens of the United States by the fourteenth amendment, and it was impossible to conjoin that status of citizenship with a total exclusion of the negro race from the ballot without undermining some of the foundation principles of our representative Republic.

Bear in mind, also, that at the time when Congress acted on that resolution in 1869, the negro had already exercised the right of suffrage under the reconstruction acts of Congress, beginning in 1867. It was not under the fifteenth amendment, but under the prior reconstruction acts, that the negroes cast their first ballots.

So that the issue then was, not whether to give the negroes something they had never possessed, but whether to deny them in the future a privilege they had already actually enjoyed.

The Southern States were expecting soon to be restored to political autonomy. What stand would the white people of those States take as to the rights of their former slaves? To what extremes of pillage and slaughter might not the millions of negroes go under fear of partial or total re-enslavement? These and other questions were hard to answer. To whatever point of the political horizon the thoughtful patriot turned his gaze, the clouds were dark and portentous. A crisis was at hand. It had to be met.

Giving the ballot to five million of newly-freed slaves, of an inferior or backward race, ignorant, unaccustomed to do or think for themselves, could not have been the deliberate act of wise statesmanship, but only the choice of what seemed to be the lesser of two evils. In truth, the whole plan seems to have been an effort not only to obliterate at once, as with a stroke of the pen, all distinctions imposed by law, but to ignore all distinctions imposed by nature.

Many thoughtful men at the North are now of the opinion that it would have been far better had the military control in the South been continued and the ballot withheld for a time, at least, from the freed man, and finally bestowed upon them by degrees. But that is a dead issue now.

As a practical measure of procedure, the fifteenth amendment was in many respects harsh and cruel toward the white people of the South, but theoretically it was necessary to round out the Constitution of a representative Republic, based on that equality of citizenship before the law which had already been foreshadowed by the thirteenth and fourteenth amendments.

We may well thank God that the South has recovered from the immediate shock of these rough post-bellum operations in political surgery. In comparison to the past —with its civil war and its reconstruction— the future can hold no terrors for us. Only let us act with wisdom and not lose what we have gained through our suffering.

Any Future Suffrage Amendment Will Increase Power of Congress.

The fifteenth amendment may, by negative acquiescence of the American people, become for a time a dead letter, but that three-fourths of the forty-five or more States will ever affirmatively repeal it for the purpose of allowing five or six Southern States to withhold from our negro citizens, as a race, the right to the ballot, is, to my mind, an hallucination too extreme for serious consideration.

If these post-bellum amendments of the Constitution bearing upon slavery shall ever be altered by future amendments, the alteration will be in the direction of placing under Federal control the entire subject of suffrage qualifications in all National and State elections. The unmistakable trend of our political and social development from the beginning of the government has been toward the centre, not away from it. The centripetal force has been stronger than the centrifugal force. Under a law of social gravitation all the parts have been drawn more intimately into one national unity.

To suppose that this national authority would of its own accord emasculate itself and surrender its own present consolidated power back to the former diverse elements from which it was wrested, would be to reverse every record of political history, and to ignore every lesson of political philosophy.

Indeed, when the resolution for the fifteenth amendment was under discussion in the Senate in 1869, an amendment to that resolution was offered to confer upon Congress the full power to prescribe the qualifications for voters and officeholders, both in the States and in the United States.

It was not adopted then because the time was not ripe. But we may accept it to be as certain as any future movement of this kind can be, that if the Constitution shall be amended on the subject of the suffrage that amendment will not restore lost power to the States, but will confer more power on the National government. The less we agitate it the better.

Numerical Relation of Races.

We have now reached the stage in our discussion

where we may best consider what is, to my mind, the most important factor in our problem, namely, the numerical relation of the whites and the blacks of the Southern States. Having the advantage in land-holdings and all other forms of wealth, in intellect, in racial pride and strength, our white supremacy can never be overthrown except by force of numbers. For many years after the war we could not rid ourselves of the apprehension that at some day in the future we might be borne down by numerical majorities. These fears were not wholly unfounded at that time.

In slavery, under the fostering care, as well as the commercial interest of the master, the negroes multiplied in a greater ratio than the whites. What effect would the new social order of freedom have on that ratio of increase? Was the Caucasian race of the South face to face with a pitiless force that might gradually but inevitably overwhelm it by sheer weight of numbers? If so, would that race yield, or would it adopt extreme measures for self-preservation? These were momentous and perturbing questions.

The census of 1870, coming first after the war, could give very little basis for deduction of any sort. But when the census figures of 1880 were made known and were compared with those of 1870, that comparison revealed a most ominous situation. Three States, South Carolina, Mississippi and Louisiana, each had at that time an actual black majority, and the per cent of gain for the negroes in the Southern group of States, as shown by the statistical experts, was far in excess of that of the whites, being 34.3, as against 27.5 per cent from all sources.

Judge Tourgee's Prophecies Not Fulfilled.

Judge Albion W. Tourgee, in his book, "An Appeal to Cæsar," published in 1884, declared that in the year 1900 every State between Maryland and Texas would have a black majority.

Time has exposed the falsity of that prediction. Not one of those States between Maryland and Texas that had a white majority in 1880 had lost it in 1900. On the contrary, every such State increased its white majority, while South Carolina, from 1890 to 1900, reduced her negro majority by 2,412, and Louisiana in the same period changed a negro majority of 798 into a white majority of 78,818.

The white majority in the ten distinctively Southern States was increased by 1,002,662 from 1890 to 1900. In the same period our white majority in Georgia rose from

119,542 to 146,481. In every Southern State, except Mississippi, where peculiar conditions prevailed, the margin of safety for white supremacy, even on the basis of numbers, has increased.

These predictions of negro majorities were not confined to writers of fiction, like Judge Tourgee. Professor Gilliam, a statistician of high repute, announced that among the whites of the old slave States the rate of natural increase from 1870 to 1880 was 20 per cent, while that of the blacks in the same States was 35 per cent.

With these figures as a basis he reached the conclusion that the 6,000,000 of Southern blacks in 1880 would increase to 12,000,000 in 1900. But when the census takers of 1900 had counted every colored man, woman and child in the whole United States, the total footed up only 8,383,-994, which is 3,616,006 less than the professor had predicted would be found in the Southern States alone.

Judge Tourgee, using these percentages, given by Professor Gilliam, argued that all the conditions pointed to a greater discrepancy in the future.

But the census of 1900 shows that the rate of increase of the blacks in the South Atlantic States, where the conditions are most favorable, was only 14.3 per cent from 1890 to 1900, instead of 35 per cent, as reported for a previous decade, while that of the whites stood substantially at its previous record of 20 per cent.

It is now an accepted fact that the census of 1870 did not give a complete enumeration of the negroes in the South, and this deficiency, by comparison with the more accurate census of 1880, necessarily showed a greater proportionate increase among the negroes than among the whites. It was this error in figures that lead to all these unfounded predictions, which for a time hung like a pall over the South.

Margin of Safety for White Supremacy Steadily Increasing.

But the census figures of 1890 and 1900 supplied the necessary data for a correct comparison. The resulting demonstration was that instead of the whites of the South being overwhelmed with a deluge of negroes, the certainty of continued white supremacy has steadily increased with every decade.

One cause of this comparative decline of the negroes in numbers is to be found in the fact that they have no source of supply from immigration, while the whites are receiving constant accessions from other States and from foreign countries. This influx of whites, comparatively small at present, will undoubtedly continue and become

31

larger with our growing industrial prosperity, which was never on so firm a foundation as now. The completion of the Panama canal will accelerate the development of our resources and give new impetus to white immigration, and thus help vastly in the solution of our problem.

A second cause of this comparative decline is that the death rate among the negroes is abnormally high. In typical Southern cities, where the death rate among the whites stands at the moderate figures of 10 to 12 per thousand, it reaches among the negroes from 20 to 25 per thousand.

It has recently been asserted by some supposedly competent authorities that the death rate of the negroes is now probably in excess of their birth rate, so that an actual numerical decrease has set in, owing largely to the ravages of consumption and certain other diseases. Nature exacts obedience to her laws—she knows neither pity nor revenge.

Professor Wilcox of Cornell University and Professor Smith of Tulane University, and others, have undertaken a more far-reaching investigation into the census figures and the facts of ethnological history, and have deduced therefrom the conclusion that "the negroes will continue to be a steadily smaller proportion of our population," and that in the course of time they will die out in America from inherent and natural causes.

Whether these extreme speculations—for they are speculations—are well founded or not, yet the established facts as to the relative increase of the races have a most important bearing on the solution of our problem. They show that this problem is not near so difficult as it was supposed to be twenty years ago, when false prophets were predicting white submergence.

And more important still, these facts show that the white people of the South, and especially of the State of Georgia, can now proceed to work out their racial problem on lines of justice to the negro, without imperilling white supremacy. Those fears which once appalled us, we may now dismiss, and let reason resume its sway.

If future years should develop enough race pride in the negroes to make them concentrate in one locality, they might gain ascendency there and give the world a practical demonstration of their capacity or incapacity as a race-force in civilization. But we see no clear signs of such a movement now, and Georgia, at least, is in no danger of being chosen as the Canaan for that sort of an experiment.

A Working Plan of Justice.

In seeking a solution of any difficult problem, the first

33

step should be to eliminate the impossible schemes proposed, and then concentrate on some line of operation that is at least possible. We often hear the epigrammatic dictum that there are but three possible solutions of our race problem: deportation, assimilation or annihilation. When we bring our sober senses to bear, all three of these so-called possibilities appear to be practical impossibilities. Not one of the three presents a working hypothesis. Physical facts, alone, prevent deportation. Physical facts, stressed by an ineradicable race pride, bar the way against assimilation. Physical facts, backed by our religion, our civilization, our very selves, forbid annihilation. We can not imitate Herod.

This much seems clear, beyond doubt, that the whites are going to stay in this Southland for all time, and so are the negroes going to stay here in greater or less proportions for generations to come. If, then, both races are to remain together, the plainly sensible thing for statesmen of this day to do is to devise the best *modus vivende*, or working plan, by which the greatest good can be accomplished for ourselves and our posterity. We of this day are not expected to overload ourselves with the burden of settling all the problems of all future ages. If we take good care of the next few centuries, we may well be content to leave some matters to be attended to by our remote posterity — aided, of course, by Providence.

Over against that Trinity of impossibilities — deportation, assimilation or annihilation — let us offer the simple plan of justice.

The first and absolutely essential factor in any working hypothesis at the South, so far as human ken can now foresee, is white supremacy — supremacy arising from present natural superiority, but based always on justice to the negro.

Those whose stock in trade is "hating the nigger" may easily gain some temporary advantage for themselves in our white primaries, where it requires no courage, either physical or moral, to strike those who have no power to strike back — not even with a paper ballot. But these men will achieve nothing permanent for the good of the State or of the nation by stirring up race passion and prejudice. Injustice and persecution will not solve any of the problems of the ages. God did not so ordain His universe.

Justly proud of our race, we refuse to amalgamate with the negro. Nevertheless, the negro is a human being, under the Fatherhood of God, and consequently within the Brotherhood of Man — for those two relations are insep-

35

arably joined together. All soul-possessing creatures must be sons of God, and joint heirs of immortality.

Moreover, the negro is an American citizen, and is protected as such, by guarantees of the Constitution that are as irrepealable almost as the Bill of Rights itself. Nor, if such a thing as repealing these guarantees were possible, would it be wise for the South. Suppose we admit the oft re-iterated proposition that no two races so distinct as the Caucasian and the negro can live together on terms of perfect equality; yet it is equally true that without some access to the ballot, present or prospective, some participation in the government, no inferior race in an elective Republic could long protect itself against reduction to slavery in many of its substantial forms—and God knows the South wants no more of that curse.

We have long passed the crisis of the disease brought on by the existence of slavery in the blood of the Republic. Let us now build up the body politic in health and strength, and guard it against ever again being inoculated with a poison even remotely resembling that deadly virus. Sporadic cases of peonage have already developed in several States and have been suppressed. Let us provide against every appearance of contagion.

Race Pride Versus Race Prejudice.

One of the most serious difficulties about the solution

of our problem is to be found in getting the dominant whites of the South to draw a proper discrimination between a laudable pride in our race, and an unworthy prejudice against the negro race. Prejudice of any sort is hostile to that sound judgment which the Creator gave us for our guide. Race prejudice presents this disturbing element in one of its most unreasoning forms. In violence it ranks next to religious fanaticism. The one is based on a supposed duty to God; the other on a supposed duty to one's race-blood. The deeper this sense of duty, the more hardened the mind against every appeal to reason. In persecuting the early Christians, Paul thought he was doing his duty to God. The men who burned the witches in New England thought they were doing their duty.

So, perhaps, may think that ex-preacher, who in our own day has turned playwright, and calling to his aid all the accessories of the stage and all the realisms of the living drama, seeks to fan into flame the fiercest passions of the whites and blacks. His chief purpose, so far as one can logically deduce it, seems to be to force into immediate conflagration combustible materials, which his heated imagination tells him must burn sometime in the future. Apparently he chafes under the delay of Providence in bringing on the ghastly spectacle, and yearns to witness with his own eyes in the flesh that reign of hell on earth before his own redeemed soul is ushered into the calm, serene and gentle presence of Him whose gospel of love and light he once preached to erring men.

If the true purpose of this reverend gentleman be to preserve the blood of our race in its purity by creating a sentiment against intermarriage of the whites and blacks, let him confine his play to Chicago and Boston and New York and Philadelphia and other like places, where some few of such marriages are said to occur. As for us in the South, we need no artificial stimulant to arouse our people against that sort of racial intermarriage. Our law forbids it, and that is one law no man or woman ever violates.

Race Purity.

In this connection let us of the South realize the hard fact that the greatest obstacle to the preservation of the purity of the blood of our race, about which we hear so much in this day, was removed when slavery was abolished. That institution, as indisputable facts too plainly show, wrought much contamination of Caucasian blood.

In Virginia in 1630 a white man-servant was publicly flogged for consorting with a negro slave, and was required to make public confession of his guilt on the following Sabbath—but clearly the custom of flogging for that offense must soon have fallen into "innocuous desuetude."

In calmly considering now the situation that confronted our statesmen of the ante-bellum period, that which most astounds us is their apparent failure to foresee what would have been the inevitable consequence of an indefinite continuance of slavery in its effect on race purity and on relative race numbers. The ratio of increase of the negroes was far in excess of the whites. The great laboring middle class, which forms the backbone of every nation's pluck and power, was fast migrating Westward, and the remaining population was rapidly crystalizing into an upper class of white slave holders and a lower class of negro slaves—the latter out-multiplying their masters in numbers. Another one hundred years of slavery would in all probability have doomed the South to absolute negro domination by mere weight of numbers whenever emancipation should come—and come it was sure to do at some time in the evolution of the elemental forces that were at work.

If there be a Providence who watches over the affairs of nations and "slumbers not nor sleeps," we may say in all reverence that he would have made an almost inex-

39

cusable blunder if he had delayed much longer the abolition of slavery.

Social recognition of the true dignity of labor, which is
so necessary to the growth of a vigorous and self-respect-
ing middle class, could not be maintained in the presence
of slavery where manual toil is so generally regarded as a
badge of servitude.

Negro Race Projected Forward Beyond Natural Development.

When a subject people in the hard school of experience gradually assert themselves and evolve from within
the physical, mental and spiritual forces that achieve their
freedom, as did the Anglo-Saxons from under the yoke of
their Norman conquerors, they come forth by natural
growth prepared for the duties and responsibilities of self-
government.

But the negro as a race had undergone no such process of evolution. His transportation from Africa to
America and his transition from slavery to freedom were
both the results of external impositions and not of internal
development. The power came from without, not from
within. He did not win his freedom. It was bestowed
upon him.

Granting that he is only a backward member of the

great human family, which as most evolutionists and Christians believe, is moving steadily on toward the distant goal of Millennial perfection, yet we cannot fail to see that the negro race was suddenly projected forward into a stage of civilization many generations in advance of its own natural development.

Is it any wonder, then, that the negro as a race should not be altogether fitted to the laws and customs and political institutions of those among whom his lot was cast?

Again, is it any wonder that this advanced civilization should find it necessary at times to apply sterner penalties for the curbing of his savage instincts when he was freed from the accustomed control of his master?

Unfortunately, soon after emancipation, some of the worst specimens of the blacks began to commit an unpardonable crime. Instantly the white man placed over the door of his home, whether it were proud mansion or humble cabin, a warning more terrible in its meaning than that which Dante dreamed he saw over the gateway to hell: "Let the brute who enters here leave all hope behind." In the presence of that crime, men do not think, they only feel.

But how shall we fix bounds for those who rush madly outside the limits of the law? Lynching began with this and similar savage crimes. But, alas, where will they all end? Let us hope that these excesses of both races are merely incidental factors in our problem, and that they will soon diminish and eventually disappear.

Abhorrent as are the crimes of some degenerate members of the negro race, we Southern people can never forget the simple faith and tragic loyalty of those thousands of slaves who guarded and protected the women and children at home, while the men were at the front fighting to drive back an invading foe whose victory meant freedom to those slaves themselves.

Negro Military Salute Confederate Monument.

Nor is there a total dearth of touching incidents in these latter days. Only about a year or so ago, a negro military company from Savannah came marching in full array up Broadway in Augusta. In front of them, rising toward the sky in beautiful, artistic proportions, stood a marble monument erected by loving women to the dead Confederacy. At its base were statues of Lee and Jackson and Cobb and Walker, and lifted high up above them all on the top of the towering shaft stood the statue of a private Confederate soldier. No white military company, no camp of maimed Confederate veterans ever pass that monument without giving it the honor of a formal salute.

42

As the negro military comes nearer, one of two gentle-tlemen standing in the doorway of a building nearby says: "Let us watch now and see if those fellows will salute the Confederate monument." The other gentleman explains that no salute will be given because it will not occur to the commanding officer, but that the omission will not be intended as an affront. Scarcely are the words spoken, when the negro captain, in clear, ringing tones that prove the sincerity of his tribute, gives the command to salute, and every black arm instantly obeys that command.

There was cheering among the white bystanders.

When the great Wade Hampton lay upon his death bed he made this prayer: "God bless all my people—white and black—God bless them all."

Suffrage Qualifications.

While the issue of political control under the fifteenth amendment still confronted the Southern States, Mississippi, having the greatest negro majority, led off with her Constitution of 1891 providing an educational qualification for voting. There being more illiterate blacks than illiterate whites in Mississippi, the necessary effect of this law was to promote white supremacy. But the law on its face did not discriminate against the negro on account of his race. It covered whites and blacks alike.

43

The Supreme Court of the United States promptly decided that this Mississippi law did not violate the Federal Constitution. What the effect of its practical administration has been need not now be discussed.

Other States followed with similar laws, based primarily on educational qualifications, but soon a proviso was evolved to preserve the ballot to illiterate whites. An honest administration of a suffrage law based on an educational qualification would necessarily disfranchise a great many whites. Hence a proviso was devised to the effect that the educational qualification should not apply to any person, nor to the descendant of any person, who could have voted at some past date, say, for example, January 1, 1867, when negroes as a class were not allowed to vote This proviso was popularly known as the "Grandfather clause," because under it, a man otherwise disqualified, might, so to speak, inherit the right of suffrage from his grandfather.

The manifest purpose of this clause was to nullify the educational requirement of the State law as to the whites, while leaving it in full force as to the negroes, and in this way to get around the 15th amendment of the Federal Constitution, which forbids discrimination on account of race.

44

The Supreme Court of the United States has gone as far as any one could have expected it to go in upholding the reserved rights of the States on the subject of suffrage. But that court has never directly nor indirectly sanctioned the validity of any suffrage law containing the Grandfather clause or any other clause based on the same principle.

Whenever the Supreme Court shall take judicial notice, as it will do, of the historical fact that on the date selected for the Grandfather clause to begin to operate, say January 1, 1867, the negroes as a class had no right to vote, or when that undeniable or easily proven fact is made to appear by evidence, this device of the Grandfather clause must fall of its own crookedness. A preference to one race is necessarily the legal equivalent of a discrimination against the other race.

It will mark a new departure in American constitutional law when the right to vote is made inheritable from the non-transmissible attributes of an ancestor instead of being based on the personal attributes of the voter.

It will mark a still further departure in judicial construction when the Supreme Court finds in this new doctrine a legal justification for sanctioning the race discrimination forbidden by the fifteenth amendment.

The Mississippi law, the only one ever squarely con-

45

sidered and directly construed by the Supreme Court, 170 U. S. 213, does not contain the Grandfather clause. That was a device of later invention.

The case of Giles *v.* Harris, 189 U. S. 475, involving the Alabama law, was dismissed in the Supreme Court for want of jurisdiction in the lower court—but Justices Brewer, Brown and Harlan dissented in vigorous terms.

The latest case, of Jones *v.* Montague, 194 U. S. 147, involving the Virginia law, was dismissed because the act sought to be enjoined—the issuing of certificates of election, etc., to members of Congress—had already been done, and the congressmen had taken their seats before the case was reached in the Supreme Court.

Indeed, it is no secret that those lawyers who undertake to defend these disfranchisement enactments, place their chief reliance in the technical difficulties of getting the merits of the question before the Supreme Court. It goes without saying, however, that lawyers can be found to surmount those technical difficulties, and at the bar of the Supreme Court confront the "Grandfather" clause of the State Constitutions with the "anti-race-discrimination" clause of the Federal Constitution.

The result scarcely admits of a doubt.

Disfranchisement Movement in Georgia.

What, then, shall we, as Georgians and Americans,

46

true to our own great State, and true to the greater nation of which it is a part, say of the movement which is now being so freely discussed, and which has seemingly gained some headway, to so amend our State Constitution as to disfranchise the negroes as a race?

We have read in the public press repeated statements that prominent leaders are openly announcing their intention to "disfranchise the negro," and promising to "eliminate him from politics." Not only so, but they further promise to accomplish that end through a so-called educational qualification or understanding clause, and at the same time not to deprive a single white man of his ballot, no matter how illiterate or ignorant he may be.

I might hesitate here and now, even at the last moment, to proceed further with the discussion of this branch of my subject if the facts as to intentions and methods, as I have just stated them, were at all in dispute. But as I understand it, there is no disposition to deny them — rather, an increasing boldness in asserting them. Therefore we may quite properly, it seems to me, proceed to draw some necessary deductions from those admitted facts as they bear on the law and morals of the situation.

How, then, are these two purposes, to put out all the negroes and put in all the whites, to be accomplished in the face of the prohibition of the fifteenth amendment? Clearly, it can not be done by open avowal in the body of the law, because in that event, the law would convict itself in any court in the land. How, then, is this avowed purpose to be accomplished? Pardon me, my friends, but let us face the truth; the scheme must be to disfranchise the negro by a fraudulent administration of the law. In no other way is it possible to produce the promised results. Legislative ingenuity must be backed up by administrative fraud—else the avowed purpose cannot be accomplished.

It must be admitted that the machinery of the proposed law could be easily perverted to fraudulent purposes. Before a citizen can register to vote, he is to be required to read and explain, or to be able to understand, any paragraph of the State Constitution. Now, we lawyers all know that there are some parts of our Constitution that the Supreme Court judges themselves have never been able fully to explain—even granting that they understand them all. But who are to judge of this explanation or understanding? The registrars, of course. Suppose the most learned explanation could be given, who will vouch that the registrars themselves will understand it, or will accept it as satisfactory?

Of course, the officers of registration are to be white.

48

An easy paragraph for a white applicant; a difficult paragraph for a negro applicant; the acceptance of any sort of an explanation from a white applicant; the rejection of any sort of an explanation from a negro applicant—there you have the hidden cards with which the game of cheat is to be played. And it is on this miserable, bare-faced scheme of fraud that our proud and noble people are asked to rest their safety and their civilization.

How long do the advocates of this method of disfranchisement think they can expose their purpose to the political eye and keep it concealed from the judicial eye? How long can they proclaim it on the hustings and hush it in the court house?

Referring to one of these laws, a learned commentator on our Supreme Court decisions has said: "If in the light of their history and conditions and the avowed purpose of the authors of the laws, their objects are clothed in statutes so worded that the real designs are not expressed in terms, the situation would seem to be one to require the court to reason from cause to effect."

The court, in construing the fourteenth amendment (118 U. S. 356) has said: "Though the law itself be fair on its face and impartial in appearance, yet if it be applied and administered by public authority with AN EVIL EYE

49

AND AN UNEQUAL HAND so as practically to make unjust and unequal discriminations between persons in similar circumstances, material to their rights, the denial of equal justice is still within the prohibition of the Constitution."

Nor can escape be found in that line of decisions by the Supreme Court to the effect that the prohibition of the fifteenth amendment applies to State action and not to acts of private citizens. The registrars who are to enforce this disfranchisement law are officers and agents of the State. The Supreme Court (100 U. S. 339) have further said: "Whoever by virtue of his public position under a State government, deprives another of life, liberty or property without due process of law, or denies or takes away the equal protection of the law, violates the inhibition of the fourteenth amendment, and as he acts in the name of, and for, the State and is clothed with her power, HIS ACT IS HER ACT."

This same principle of responsibility will be applied to the registrars under this disfranchisement law. Their acts will be the acts of the State, and will consequently come within the prohibition of the fifteenth amendment, and will also be within the jurisdiction of the Federal courts, where alleged violations of the law will be tried.

But aside from these legal aspects of the matter, let us

ask ourselves if there is not a more serious practical difficulty to be overcome. These registrars, as officers, must take the usual oath to perform their duties impartially under the law. Let us put the plain, blunt question: How many counties in Georgia can be relied on to furnish three citizens for registrars who will agree in advance to violate their solemn oaths? Will not honest men point at them the finger of scorn?

The great John C. Calhoun sought to nullify a Federal statute law on the tariff by State action because he believed it to be in violation of the Federal Constitution, which he loved and honored.

But these latter day nullifiers are seeking to nullify the Federal Constitution by a State law—no, not by a State law itself, but by the fraudulent administration of a State law. No power on earth could have made Mr. Calhoun stoop to such chicanery—he was fashioned in a nobler mould. What a contrast between the great nullifier and these little nullifiers!

The abuses to which the broad discretionary powers of the registrars under these disfranchisement laws might be carried in times of fierce partisan politics are absolutely unlimited. We need not flatter ourselves that white men will never be the victims of such abuses. When moral

51

character is once defiled and fraud seeks its own selfish ends, it will not stop at the color line.

One Danger in Educational Qualification.

There can be no legal objection, whenever the public necessity requires it, to establishing a reasonable educational qualification for voters, provided that qualification is fairly and honestly applied. But if this educational qualification is to be used as a fraudulent subterfuge to disfranchise the negro, then there is another very serious consequence which will necessarily follow.

If by appeals to race prejudice and fear these negro disfranchisers establish the educational test in fulfilment of their promise to "eliminate the negro from politics," then of necessity, these same leaders and their followers must recognize that from their point of view it is not the IGNORANT, but the EDUCATED negroes who will be the most dangerous political enemies of the whites.

The question will at once arise, why should the white people create dangerous political enemies by allowing the negroes to be educated? Why not "eliminate them from politics" by keeping them in ignorance? There is no escape from the logic of this argument if the premise be correct. Thus we would find ourselves committed to the degrading policy of enforcing ignorance on a weaker race, with its attendant results of peonage and semi-slavery, from which all good men would pray for deliverance.

Division of School Funds on Race Lines.

Even now there are signs of a movement in Georgia to give the negro schools only that pittance of money arising from the negro's taxes. A law to that effect has already been declared invalid by the State court in North Carolina (94 N. C. 709); also by the State court in Kentucky (83 Ky. 49); and also by the Federal court in three decisions from Kentucky (16 Fed. R. p. 297; 23 Fed. R. 634, and 72 Fed R. 689.)

In our own State a bill to the same effect was passed in 1888 for a local school system, and Governor John B. Gordon, while Hon. Clifford Anderson was attorney general, vetoed it on the ground that it was against sound policy and a violation of the Constitution of the State and the United States.

There is nothing in the decision of our State Supreme Court in the Eatonton case (80 Ga. 755) nor in the Richmond County High School case (103 Ga. 641) to sustain the proposition that the common school funds of the State, or of any subdivision of the State, can be divided between the races in proportion to the property or taxes of each. On the contrary, in the latter case, our State court said:

"So far as the record discloses, both races have the same facilities of attending them" (the free common schools). And the United States Supreme Court, in reviewing this Georgia case (175 U. S. 528) say it is an admitted principle of law that the "benefits and burdens of public taxation must be shared by citizens without discrimination against any class on account of their race."

Along this same line spoke Governor Charles J. Jenkins, known to Georgians as the "Noblest Roman of Them All," when he took the chair as president of the Constitutional convention of 1877. He said:

"I utter no caution against class legislation or discrimination against our citizens of African descent. I feel a perfect assurance that there is no member of this body who would propose such action, and if there were, he would soon find himself without a following."

These are the words of a high-minded statesman — not of a time-serving politician. There are many differences between these two types of public men. One difference is that a politician seeks to find out what public opinion is and hastens to follow it, while a statesman seeks to find out what public opinion ought to be and helps to mould it.

Our late Chancellor Hill, whose untimely death is so deeply deplored by us all, belonged to that higher class of moulders of public opinion. By example, as well as by precept, he led the way to the nobler ends of life.

Should Georgia Follow Other States?

Surely nothing but the direst necessity of self-preservation could induce any people to resort to such suffrage expedients as are now being proposed to the people of Georgia. Nothing less than an impending overthrow of white civilization by negro domination could excuse such extreme measures. But if our discussion has shown anything, it has shown that Georgia is not now in danger of negro domination.

One argument that is being pressed upon our people is that Georgia should follow the example of other Southern States that have passed similar disfranchisement laws. But let us ask, why should Georgia follow them? Is there anything in their examples on this subject worthy of our imitation? If their necessities compelled such questionable action, let us sympathize with them in their extremity. But let us not imitate them when no such necessity besets us. Did not Georgia first redeem herself after reconstruction? Has she not kept abreast of her sister States in material, intellectual and moral progress? Is she not still the Empire State of the South? What State can show a a cleaner official record for thirty years? Rather let

Georgia continue to lead in wise and conservative states-manship. On all fundamental questions our white people are sufficiently united in thought and purpose to come together in a solid phalanx if the negroes should ever return to the ballot box in sufficient numbers on one side of an issue to jeopardize the public safety.

As a legal means of maintaining white supremacy, no plan yet devised approaches in effectiveness our party primary system, in combination with the cumulative poll tax provision of the Constitution.

Whatever may be the final political status of the negro, we are now undeniably in a transition stage of evolution. It is scarcely conceivable that the conditions created by the disfranchisement laws of some Southern States can be permanent. The battle for supremacy between those laws and the Federal Constitution remains to be fought out. If the Federal Constitution proves victorious, as it is very apt to do, then the entire electoral system of these States may have to be changed.

On the other hand, Georgia, through her superior statesmanship, has put herself in a position of safety, ready to take advantage of whatever hopeful developments the future may unfold. She has violated no Federal law.

She has maintained white supremacy with the least possible friction, and can continue to so maintain it.

Not only is this campaign against the negro unnecessary and unjust, but it is most inopportune at this juncture. When every County in the State is calling loudly for more labor to serve the household and till the fields and develop our resources, why should we seek to enact more oppressive laws against the labor we now have?

We do not know what shifting phases this vexing race problem may assume, but we may rest in the conviction that its ultimate solution must be reached by proceeding along the lines of honesty and justice. Let us not in cowardice or in want of faith, needlessly sacrifice our higher ideals of private and public life. Race differences may necessitate social distinctions. But race differences can not repeal the moral law.

The Moral Law—Its Origin and Sanction.

What is this thing we call the moral law? Is it a mere weak sentiment, suitable only for children and preachers and Sunday school teachers? Or is it the fiat of Nature and Nature's God, commanding obedience from all men under the sanction of inevitable penalties? We will waive all questions as to weight of authority, and reason out the matter for ourselves.

Whence come our morals or ethical conceptions? Briefly let us summarize:

First: The theological school rests the foundation of morals on divine commandment or revelation, which quickens the conscience.

God spake through Moses, the Prophets and the Christ.

Second: The psychological school traces the source of morals to an instinct or sense that is innate in the mind itself—the conscience.

The philosopher and metaphysician, Immanuel Kant, reasoned back to his celebrated postulate of a "categorical imperative" call to duty.

Third: The utilitarian school evolves morals from human experience, sanctioning as "good" or "right" that conduct which has proven beneficial, and condemning as "bad" or "wrong" that conduct which has proven injurious, thus creating and developing the conscience by successive stages of experimental knowledge.

Herbert Spencer thus evolved his system of utilitarian ethics till it almost flowered out in the beauty of the "Golden Rule."

Professor Huxley, discussing the scientific doctrine of causation, says: "The safety of morality lies in a real and living belief in that fixed order of nature which sends social disorganization upon the track of immorality as surely as it sends physical disease after physical trespassers."

It is not necessary for us to determine how much of truth there is in each of these schools of thought. Enough for us to know that all three reach substantially the same conclusion as to right rules of conduct for men. By different routes they arrive at the same goal. In reasoning they are three; in acting they are one. Here is a subject on which religion and science are in full accord, namely, that the moral law is the wisest rule of human conduct.

So much for the individual man.

The Moral Law Applies to States as Well as to Individuals.

Now, does the same moral law apply to States and Nations as well as to individuals? Or are there two codes of morality, one for individuals and another for aggregations of individuals? Can we practice fraud as a collective body of citizens and still preserve our personal integrity as individual citizens?

We might quote Mr. Jefferson as an authority for the doctrine that "moral duties are as obligatory on nations as on individuals." But again let us waive authority and reason out our own conclusions. We will test the question

59

by the standards of the three schools of thought first named.

If we assume that the theological school is correct, it is manifest that there can not be a code of public morals different in principle from the code of private morals. God must deal with individuals and nations alike, because the former are the responsible units of the latter.

If we assume that the psychological school is correct, it is equally manifest that the conscience, being an innate mental quality, cannot reverse its action by changing from private to public capacity, from individual to collective functions.

If we assume that the utilitarian school is correct, it ought to be equally as clear that the rule of conduct which experience has proven to be beneficial as between individuals, is also beneficial as between States under like conditions.

It is true that aggregations of individuals, by reason of divided responsibility, do not usually act up to the code of morals recognized by single individuals. That historical fact shows the imperfection of our past civilization, and calls upon us for better work in the future. No one accepts the condition as permanent or satisfactory. The great task of civilization, the dearest hope of philosophers and noble-minded statesmen, is to constantly improve that condition and bring nations more under the sway of the moral law. Though perfection be unattainable, every step is progress.

In proportion as international intercourse becomes more free will a code of international ethics, based on a code of personal ethics, be developed, to the immeasurable advantage of all concerned. Such is the doctrine underlying The Hague tribunal, which has already done so much for the peace of the world.

One of the noblest tributes ever paid to Gladstone was that he had applied the moral law to British politics.

It was Aristides, surnamed the Just—a brave soldier, a successful general, a man of sound practical judgment, not a mere dreamer—who, when named by the Athenians to consider a secret plan, suggested by Thermistocles, to gain naval supremacy for Athens by burning the ships of her allies, reported against the unscrupulous scheme and said: "What Thermistocles proposes might be to your present advantage, but O Athenians, it is not just."

Speaking of the ideal, universal, moral code, one of the least sentimental of modern scientific writers says: "Although its realization may lie in the unseen future, civilization must hold fast to it, if it would be any more than a blind natural process; and it is certainly the noblest function of social science to point out the wearisome way along which mankind, dripping with blood, yet pants for the distant goal."

Another deep thinker, summing up the facts of history and the reasonings of philosophers, says: "That the moral law is the unchanging law of social progress in human society is the lesson which appears to be written over all things."

Solution of Race Problem: Give Negro Justice.

The foundation of the moral law is justice. Let us solve the negro problem by giving the negro justice and applying to him the recognized principles of the moral law.

This does not require social equality. It does not require that we should surrender into his inexperienced and incompetent hands the reins of political government. But it does require that we recognize his fundamental rights as a man, and that we judge each individual according to his own qualifications, and not according to the lower average characteristics of his race. Political rights can not justly be withheld from those American citizens of an inferior or backward race who raise themselves up to the standard of

62

citizenship which the superior race applies to its own members.

It is true that the right of suffrage is not one of those inalienable rights of man, like life, liberty and the pursuit of happiness, as enumerated in the Declaration of Independence, but the right of exemption from discrimination in the exercise of suffrage on account of race, is one of the guaranteed constitutional rights of all American citizens.

We of the South are an integral part of this great country. We should stand ready to make every sacrifice demanded by honor and permitted by wisdom to remove the last vestige of an excuse for the perpetuation of that spirit of sectionalism which excludes us from the full participation in governmental honors to which our brain and character entitles us.

Let us respect the National laws to the limit of endurance, and if that limit should be passed, let us resort to some means of redress more typical of Southern manhood than fraudulent subterfuge. The future material prosperity of the South is already assured. Let us resolve that there shall remain ingrained in the moral fibre of our New South the high character of our Old South—which can best be described in the memorable words of Edmund

Burke as "that sensibility of principle, that chastity of honor which felt a stain like a wound."

We cannot afford to sacrifice our ideas of justice, of law and of religion for the purpose of preventing the negro from elevating himself. If we wish to preserve the wide gap between our race and his in the onward progress of civilization, let us do it by lifting ourselves up, not by holding him down.

If, as some predict, the negro in the distant future must fail and fall by the wayside in the strenuous march of the nations, let him fall by his own inferiority, and not by our tyranny. Give him a fair chance to work out what is in him.

Carl McKinley, that brilliant and noble-hearted author of "An Appeal to Pharoah," who advocated so earnestly and so eloquently the impracticable policy of deportation, declared himself on this subject as follows:

"We should have learned by this time moreover, that we cannot treat the negro with injustice, however disguised, without sharing the consequences with him. * * * It would be a foul wrong to beat him back in his upward struggle, and consign him to a lower plane and establish him on it."

If the negro as a race is to be disfranchised regardless

of the personal qualifications of meritorious individual members of that race, consider for a moment some of the changes we must make in many of the fundamental doctrines lying at the base of our government. The revised version of our political Bible would have to read something like this: "No taxation without representation — except as to negroes;" "equal rights to all — except as to negroes;" "all men are created equal — except as to negroes."

No Recantation of Jefferson's Doctrine.

Some modern critics seriously suggest that we should amend that paragraph of the Declaration of Independence which asserts the equal rights of men, so as to adjust it more accurately to historical and scientific facts. But that epoch-making document needs no alteration upon the subject of human rights when interpreted as it was intended to be interpreted by the man who drafted it. Mark you, Mr. Jefferson did not write "All men are born free," as the quotation is sometimes given. That looser language is found in the Constitution of Massachusetts, not in the Declaration of Independence. Such an assertion would have been disproved by the historical fact of slavery then existing. What Mr. Jefferson wrote was: "All men are created equal." That is to say, not equal in exterior circumstances, nor in physical or mental attributes, but equal in the sight of God and just human law, in their alienable rights to life, liberty and the pursuit of happiness. Americans want no recantation of that declaration. It is the political corollary of the Christian doctrine of the justice and the Fatherhood of God. Let it stand as it was penned by Jefferson, an ennobling, even though unattainable, ideal, demanded by the spiritual nature of man—one of those ideals that have done more to lift up humanity and to build up civilization than all the gold from all the mines of all the world.

www.ingramcontent.com/pod-product-compliance
Lightning Source LLC
Chambersburg PA
CBHW072111280526
45788CB00006B/2494